THEN AND TH
GENERAL EDIT
MARJORIE RE

Napoleon and the French Empire

DAVID SYLVESTER

Illustrated from contemporary sources

LONGMAN

LONGMAN GROUP LIMITED
London
*Associated companies, branches and representatives
throughout the world*

First published 1978
ISBN 0 582 20546 8

Printed in Hong Kong
by Wilture Enterprises (International) Ltd.

For Adam, Jan, Jacob and Benjamin

Contents

To the Reader

If you had grown up in Britain between 1800 and 1815 you would certainly have heard the name of Napoleon or Bonaparte. Everyone talked about him. In the House of Commons politicians debated how they could stop him and his armies. Songs were made up about him and heard in town and country. Even mothers settled their children by saying that if they were not quiet or did not go to sleep 'Boney would get them'. A nursery rhyme went:

> Baby, baby, naughty baby,
> Hush, you squalling thing I say,
> Hush your squalling, or it may be
> Bonaparte will pass this way.
>
> Boney, Boney, he's a giant,
> Tall and black as Rouen steeple,
> And he dines and sups, rely on't,
> Every day on naughty people.

If you had grown up in France at the same time you too would have heard the name Napoleon on everyone's lips. Here, however, the talk would have been of the great battles he had won and the glories he had brought to France. In this book you will read how Napoleon became such a giant figure in the age in which he lived, and something, too, about what it was like to live under the shadow of his Grand French Empire.

Words printed in *italics* are explained in the Glossary on page 93.

1 Rising Ambition

One mid-October day in 1795 a fourteen-year-old boy, Eugène de Beauharnais, was allowed into the military headquarters in Paris to see General Napoleon Bonaparte, second in command of the French Army. The Government had recently ordered that all weapons were to be given up to the army and the boy had come to ask permission to keep his father's sword. Alexandre de Beauharnais, the boy's father, had once been commander of the Army of the Rhine in 1793, but he had been unsuccessful in war and had been sentenced to death. The boy wanted the sword as a keepsake: General Bonaparte kindly agreed to his request.

Eugène de Beauharnais must have left the headquarters in a happy mood. He was proud of his father and glad to be able to keep his sword. What he did not know was that he had just met his future stepfather and a man who was to be the giant figure in Europe for the next twenty years.

Napoleon Bonaparte was born on 15 August 1769 in Corsica, the son of a Corsican nobleman. The year before, the Genoese had sold the island to France, and under their leader Paoli, the Corsicans tried to resist the French. But by August 1769 they had been defeated and Paoli had gone into exile in England. Napoleon's father, who fought with Paoli, decided to make his peace with the French. He soon obtained an important job working for the French government and became particularly friendly with de Marboeuf, the French Governor of Corsica. This friendship was important for the young Napoleon because in 1780, when he was nine, it was de

Marboeuf who recommended his admission to the Military School at Brienne. Napoleon's army career had begun.

At Brienne Napoleon showed himself to be specially good at mathematics and so in 1784, when he went on to the Ecole Militaire (Military School) at Paris, it was decided that he should enter not the *infantry* but the *artillery* where mathematical skill counted. His examination results in one year were so good that he jumped the lower grades and was immediately made a lieutenant. At the end of 1785, when he was fifteen, he joined his first regiment at Valence in the Rhône Valley.

The young Napoleon

When the French Revolution broke out in 1789 Napoleon welcomed it mainly because he thought it would bring freedom for his native island of Corsica. Paoli had returned there and Napoleon became one of his supporters until June 1793 when, after a quarrel between Paoli and the Bonaparte family, the Bonapartes were forced to leave Corsica and go and live in France. From then on Napoleon forgot his dreams for Corsica and decided to seek his fortune by serving France and the Revolution.

Since October 1792 the National Convention had ruled France. The King, Louis XVI, was *guillotined* on 21 January 1793 and on 1 February war was declared against Britain and Holland. Soon France was at war with all Europe, apart from Switzerland and the Scandinavian countries. There was also danger of civil war at home.

Napoleon applied for a post in the Army of the Rhine but chance took him to Toulon in the west. There the dead King's supporters had welcomed a British fleet into the port and a French revolutionary army was besieging the town. When the officer commanding the artillery in the French army was wounded, Napoleon was sent to replace him. Immediately he became one of the leaders in the attack. By 18 December the British were forced out of Toulon and although Napoleon received a thigh wound from a British bayonet in the course of the final assault, his commanders had noted his skill. In February 1794 he was promoted brigadier-general and in March he was posted to the army in Italy as artillery commander.

At the beginning of October 1795 the French Government was desperately in need of an energetic general. Paris had risen in rebellion and Barras, Commander of the *Army of the Interior*, looked round for someone to help him crush the rebels. He had seen Napoleon in action at Toulon: here was his man. The Convention had about 5,000 troops against the rebel force of some 25,000 men. Napoleon placed his troops carefully, sent the young Captain Murat to bring cannon, and as soon as his artillery arrived fired point-blank at the rebels on the steps of Saint Roch Church. This 'whiff of grapeshot' was immediately effective. Three or four hundred were killed and the remainder ran away. The 'Vendémiaire' crisis (3-5 October 1795) was over. Napoleon was promoted to major-general and soon after succeeded Barras as commander of the   7

Army of the Interior. So it was that when young Eugène de Beauharnais visited the army headquarters in the Rue des Capucines to ask for his father's sword he was ushered into the presence of General Bonaparte.

Soon after, Eugène's mother, Joséphine de Beauharnais, called on Bonaparte to thank him for his kindness and this meeting led to a brief courtship during which Napoleon fell madly in love. On 9 March 1796 Joséphine and Napoleon were married. Two days later Napoleon left Paris to take up his new office as Commander of the Army of Italy.

When Napoleon arrived at Nice on 27 March many *veteran* officers welcomed him. He was not particularly striking to look at. He was a rather pale, thin man with long, lank hair reaching down to his shoulders and ill-fitting boots and clothes. He was also below average in height. But even if his figure was not very dashing, he arrived in Italy with a reputation for being a general who could make successful decisions, and this is what the troops in Italy wanted. Moreover, he knew how to appeal to the ordinary soldier. He talked to them and made them feel that he cared for them. As soon as he arrived in Italy he thrilled his men with speeches like this:

> Soldiers you are half starved and half naked. The Government owes you much, but can do nothing for you. Your patience and courage are honourable to you but they bring you neither gain nor glory. I am about to lead you into the most *fertile* valleys of the world. There you will find flourishing cities and *teeming* provinces. There you will reap honour, glory and riches. Soldiers of the Army of Italy, will you lack courage?

In Italy the French were faced by some 30,000 Austrian troops and about 12,000 troops from Piedmont. Napoleon decided that the best plan was to separate these two enemy forces. First he crushed the Piedmontese in the battle of Mondovi. Next he pursued the Austrians. He crossed the river Po at Piacenza

Opposite: *Napoleon attacking the rebels at Saint Roch Church*

and came upon the enemy rearguard at Lodi (see the map on p. 21). Here the Austrians had placed a battery of thirty cannon to stop the French crossing the wooden bridge. Seeing this, one French officer said: 'It is impossible that any men can force their way across that narrow bridge, in the face of such a storm of cannon balls.' 'Impossible!' exclaimed Napoleon, 'that word is not French.' He set up his own French artillery and began to return the enemy fire. Then, when the battle was at its height he dashed to the front to position two guns so that they covered the only path which the Austrians could use to set mines under the bridge and explode it. Napoleon's bravery in exposing himself to the enemy fire won him the respect of his soldiers and also the nickname of 'the Little Corporal'. It showed that the soldiers considered Napoleon to be one of them, and it was because of this that they followed him.

On 10 May the French took the bridge at Lodi and defeated the Austrians. Later Napoleon talked of his victory as a turning point in his career. He had always wanted to get to the top but he had often despaired of ever doing so. Now, after Lodi, he was much more sure of himself. Later he wrote: 'It was only on the evening after Lodi that I realised I was a superior being and thought out the ambition of performing great things, which hitherto had filled my thoughts only as a *fantastic* dream.'

In 1797 success came again. On 15 January he caught the Austrian army at Rivoli, as it made one more attempt to relieve Mantua. He routed it completely and then hurried back in time to force the surrender of another Austrian relief force coming from Padua to Mantua.

By March Napoleon's army had received reinforcements from France giving him a total of 80,000 men, and he decided to advance on the Archduke Charles who was gathering the Austrian forces together again at Friuli. The Austrians retreated in his path but Napoleon, realising that he could be easily attacked from behind, decided to propose a peace. This was finally confirmed in the Treaty of Campo Formio on

18 October 1797. France was to keep her frontier on the Rhine and also control the part of Italy from Rome to Lombardy.

Napoleon had achieved much both for France and for himself; he had also pointed to the future for both. For France he had seen the way to further conquest beyond her 'natural frontiers' of the Rhine, the Pyrenees and the Alps, into Italy and elsewhere. This would mean war and a constant call upon France to provide young men for her armies. In return France would get glory and new possessions. A start had already been made, for as well as getting more land, much treasure had been gained in gold and silver and in the splendid pictures which had been sent back to Paris to hang with many others in the Louvre palace.

In May 1797 Napoleon had been joined in Italy by his wife Joséphine and here he began to act like a king. A visitor to

Joséphine de Beauharnais

11

Milan described what Napoleon's court was like:

> I was received by Bonaparte in the midst of a brilliant court rather than the headquarters of an army. Strict *etiquette* already reigned around him; his *aides-de-camp* and his officers were no longer received at his table, and he had become *fastidious* in the choice of the guests whom he admitted to it. An invitation was an honour eagerly sought and obtained with great difficulty. He dined, so to speak, in public; the inhabitants of the country were admitted to the room in which he was eating, allowed to gaze at him with a keen curiosity. . . . His reception rooms and an immense tent pitched in front of the palace were constantly full of a crowd of generals, *administrators*, and big contractors; besides members of the highest nobility in Italy who came to ask the favour of a momentary glance or the briefest interview.

Napoleon was for the present merely acting the part of a king, but already the idea of seizing power had occurred to him. He told this visitor that he had not conquered Italy for the French Government but for his 'own profit'. However, he decided that the right moment had not yet come to make himself king. He was playing a waiting game.

2 *Grasping Power*

Paris gave Napoleon a hero's welcome and the Rue Chantereine where he lived was renamed Rue de la Victoire. Napoleon, however, chose to lead a quiet life outside politics and he gave no hint of his ambitions. He took off his uniform and appeared in ordinary clothes. He was seen mainly in the company of scientists and writers. He knew, however, that he must do something which would keep him in the public eye. 'In Paris,' he said 'nothing is remembered for long. If I continue doing nothing I am finished.' He was offered command of the Invasion Army of England but he thought the invasion plan was impossible and rejected it. He suggested instead an expedition to Egypt. The aim was to damage British trade by stopping her merchants going through Egypt to and from India.

This appealed to the Government. They were afraid of Napoleon and this plan would get him out of the way. Moreover, if it succeeded, it would help to cripple the British, with whom the French were at war. On 19 May 1798 Napoleon set sail for Egypt. He took thirteen warships and almost 400 transport ships carrying some 38,000 troops. But it was more than a military expedition. Napoleon wanted to make a new French territory, so he took with him over 150 scientists, engineers and *archaeologists*, with their books, tools and instruments to study and survey the land.

He disembarked his troops and on 2 July took Alexandria. He then marched on to Cairo and on 21 July defeated the *cavalry* of the Turkish rulers of Egypt.

Despite his victory Napoleon had mixed feelings about 13

The Battle of the Pyramids, 21 July 1798

being in Egypt. On 25 July 1798 he wrote to his brother Joseph:

> The papers will tell you about the result of the fighting and the conquest of Egypt. There was enough resistance to add a glorious page to the military *annals* of the army. Egypt is the richest country in the world for corn, rice, meat, vegetables. It is as *barbarous* as it can be. There is no money, not even enough to pay the troops. I may be in France again in two months. Please look after my interests. . . . I am tired of glory at twenty-nine; it has lost its charm. . . . I mean to keep my Paris house — I shall never give that up to anyone.

Soon after, on 1 August, the English fleet under Admiral Nelson caught the French fleet in Aboukir Bay and completely destroyed it. Napoleon was now left stranded without support from the sea. He tried to win over the native Arab population by stopping his troops from *plundering* and by setting up native advisory councils in Cairo and in the provinces. He also showed great respect for the religion of *Islam*. He founded an institute of Egypt which was to be a centre where scholars could study the land and he started plans for archaeological and geographical explorations.

In January 1799 Napoleon heard that the Governor of Syria was raising an army to attack him. He decided to counter this by making the first move himself, so he marched into Palestine and took the port of Jaffa on 7 March. Here he showed two different sides of his character. On the one hand he acted like a real leader. When plague broke out in the army, he bravely mingled with his soldiers to revive their courage. On the other hand, he showed himself to be quite ruthless. Some 3,000 Turkish prisoners had been captured and Napoleon had them *massacred* on the grounds that he had no food to feed them. The real reason was probably that he wanted to discourage any others who might be thinking of taking up arms against him. But whatever the reason it is a blot on Napoleon's greatness. A good leader he may have been but he could also be a heartless butcher of men. Napoleon's assistant paymaster left this account of what happened:

> About 3,000 men put down their arms and were instantly led to our camp. By order of the Commander-in-Chief, the Egyptians, Moroccans, and Turks were separated.
> The next morning, all the Moroccans were taken down to the sea-shore, and two battalions began to shoot them down. Their only hope of saving their lives was to throw themselves into the sea; they did not hesitate, and all tried to escape by swimming. They were shot at leisure, and soon the sea was red with blood and covered with corpses. A few were lucky enough to reach some rocks. Soldiers were ordered to follow them in boats and to finish them off. . . . Once this execution was over, we hoped that it

15

would not be repeated and that the other prisoners would be spared. . . . Our hopes were soon disappointed, when the next day, 1,200 Turkish artillerymen who for two days had been kept without food in front of General Bonaparte's tent, were taken to be executed. The soldiers had been carefully instructed not to waste ammunition, and they were ferocious enough to stab them with their bayonets. Among the victims, we found many children who, in the act of death, had clung to their fathers.

After this Napoleon went on to Acre, confident and with every hope of new triumphs. It was not to be. Reinforced by a small English naval squadron the garrison at Acre successfully resisted Napoleon's two-month *siege*. The only thing he could do was return to Cairo.

Here he had better fortune. Almost immediately he wiped out his defeat in Syria by a complete victory at Aboukir on 25 July 1799. Once again it seemed that his dream of an empire in the east was possible. News from France of French defeats in Italy and on the Rhine, however, turned Napoleon's mind back to Europe. He thought perhaps the moment had come for him to make his bid for power. The Government would obviously be unpopular with the mass of the people. France would be looking for a saviour, and Napoleon was very willing to play the part.

On 24 August Napoleon left Egypt for Paris and was greeted everywhere by enthusiastic crowds. There were some in the Government, however, who were not at all pleased to see him back. Some wanted him thrown out of the army for leaving his post in Egypt. But a small group found in Napoleon just what they had been looking for. Three ministers in the Government had decided to seize power for themselves. They were looking for a soldier to help them and Napoleon appeared just at the right time.

Opposite: *The members of one of the Government Councils attack Napoleon*

On 9 November 1799 the Councils of the Government were persuaded to move out of Paris on the excuse that it would protect them from a plot, and Napoleon was given command of the troops in Paris. The next day the Councils began to question why they had been moved and Napoleon decided to intervene and appear before the Councils himself. Unfortunately for him, his speech to one Council was a disaster which he made worse at the end by saying that if anyone suggested that he was acting outside the law, he would appeal to 'his brave companions in arms', his soldiers. This angered the Council members so much that Napoleon had to leave the chamber. He now tried to interrupt the debates of the other Council, but as soon as he appeared he was surrounded and pushed and punched by its angry members.

Once he had gone, the Council called for a vote to outlaw Napoleon. Fortunately for him, his brother Lucien was President of the Council and he refused to put it to the vote. Mounted on his horse Napoleon rode among the ranks of the guards appealing to them with the story, 'I went to speak to them and they answered me with dagger blows'. A column of grenadiers, led by General Murat, entered the hall with fixed bayonets, and the members fled. In the evening those members of the Councils who remained agreed to end the present Government.

Napoleon had done badly in the *coup d'état*. It was his brother Lucien who saved the day, and Napoleon was lucky to hold his own position. However, in the following months he gradually persuaded more members to support him so that when the *Constitution* finally appeared he was given the position of First Consul, and the other two consuls were very much under his thumb. Indeed, as the various Councils in the Government were all chosen by the consuls, Napoleon had complete power.

In February 1800 a vote of the French people approved the new Constitution and agreed by over 3 million votes for to only 1,500 against what was, in fact, Napoleon's seizure of power.

3   Peace Abroad

Napoleon had seized power but he knew that he would keep it only if he kept the French people contented. At that time the French wanted peace at home and a victorious peace in Europe.

First, Napoleon decided to try to gain victory on the battle-field. This, he knew, would make him a hero with the people and if a good peace could be made to follow it, then he would have time to make a better government inside France itself.

His plan was brilliant but difficult to achieve. There were two French armies in the field. Moreau was commanding the Army of the Rhine, and the Army of Italy was trying hard to hold off the Austrians in Genoa. Napoleon decided that the Army of the Rhine must stay where it was. He himself would take the Army of Reserve, and cross the Alps to catch the Austrians, who were besieging Genoa (see the map on p. 21), from behind.

Napoleon planned this campaign in great excitement. He wanted the name of Bonaparte to go down in history with a blaze of glory and what better way could there be than to do it by crossing the Alps into Italy as the great Carthaginian general Hannibal had done so many hundreds of years before (about 219 B.C.). An army of 60,000 men prepared for the journey; most of them were raw recruits, and only about a third of them had ever fired a shot in battle before.

The army set out on 27 April 1800 for the Great St Bernard Pass in the Alps. An Austrian garrison covered the end of the Pass. As Napoleon's advance guard approached, great guns opened fire and the French had to form a single file to escape

Napoleon's army crossing the Great St Bernard Pass

their shot. The artillery were not so fortunate: many of the cannons were blasted to bits and only ten out of forty got through. However, the march was a great success. It caught the Austrians by surprise and on 2 June Napoleon entered Milan (see the map opposite).

He now decided to advance quickly westwards and try to meet the main Austrian army. As he was anxious to find them, he took a great risk and split his forces. He sent two divisions under Désaix, south of the River Po, and another to the north. But far from finding the enemy, it was the Austrians who found Napoleon. On 14 June his advance guard was suddenly attacked by the Austrians at Marengo. They faced him in the open plain with 30,000 men and ninety-three guns. Napoleon had only 22,000 men and fifteen guns.

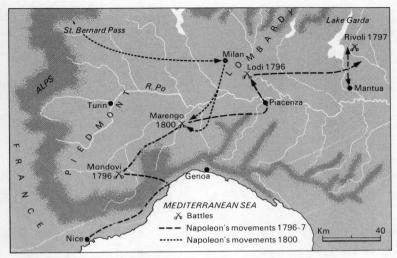

Napoleon's two Italian campaigns

He immediately recalled his other divisions. He tried to re-organise his forces but was unable to prevent their disorderly retreat. Fortunately Desaix arrived with a force of 5,000 men and five cannon. Desaix attacked the front of the Austrian column. Soon after Kellermann arrived with 400 cavalry and charged the Austrian flank. Unexpectedly, these two efforts made the Austrians panic and turned their advance into retreat and Napoleon gained the victory he wanted, though had it not been for Desaix, who was killed in leading the counter-attack, the outcome and future history might have been very different.

The battle of Marengo was a turning point for Napoleon. As a result of victory over the Austrians, France was given the entire left bank of the Rhine, including Belgium and Luxembourg. She also took control of central and northern Italy. The next year Britain made peace with France.

Napoleon had given France the first thing he had been aiming at, a victorious peace. He was now free to turn to his other aim of trying to give the French people a peaceful and orderly country in which to live.

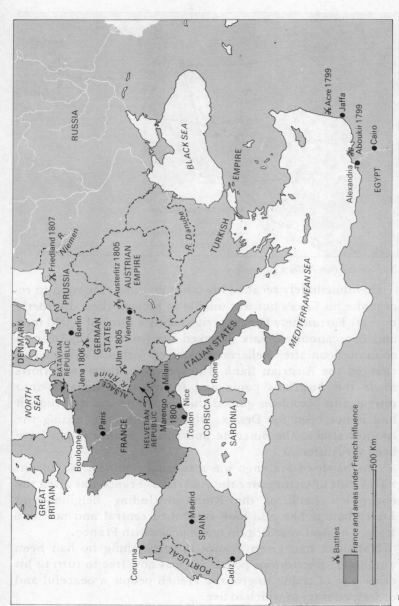

Europe in 1801, and showing Napoleon's main battles up to 1807

4   Peace at Home

Napoleon realised that he must show the French that he was not only a good soldier, but also a good ruler. Otherwise he would not survive. On 24 December 1800 there had been an attempt to kill him. Explosives had been hidden in a cart in the Rue Saint-Nicaise on the route he was to take from the Tuileries Palace to the Opera. It was only by seconds that Napoleon and Joséphine escaped the explosion, which killed and injured many bystanders.

The incident reminded Napoleon that being a victorious general was not enough.

HIS GOVERNMENT

First, he planned to do all the governing from one place. Previous revolutionary governments had allowed the provinces and country districts to settle a lot of their affairs without asking the central government in Paris. Napoleon changed all this. The Constitution of the Consulate, as you have seen, gave all the supreme power to the First Consul, who was Napoleon. It was true that all adult men had the right to vote and elect a national list of about 6,000 men from whom the members of the various governing councils were chosen but it was Napoleon and his fellow consuls who did the choosing. They chose the members of the *Senate*, the *Tribunal* of 100 which discussed laws but could not change them, and the *Legislative* of 300 which could not discuss but merely pass or reject laws. In 1790 the old provinces of France had been replaced by new *administrative districts* (called Departments) with their own elected councils. In 1800 Napoleon replaced these with

23

The attempt to kill Napoleon at the Rue Saint-Nicaise

officials called prefects, appointed by the First Consul and
having complete charge of the Departments. Moreover, the
various councils of the Department and local mayors were to
be chosen by the central government. The prefects were
Napoleon's agents in the provinces, completely under his
control.

At the centre of the government was Napoleon himself,
helped by a Council of State which was divided into five
sections to deal with war, the navy, home affairs, law-making
and finance (money). One reason for Napoleon's success as a
governor was that he was clever enough to pick out the best of
the men who had ruled in the past, and had the sense to rely
on them and pick their brains. He sat at the head of this
Council and let it discuss affairs freely, although in the end he

24

made the decisions himself. He alone could appoint and dismiss councillors, so the Council was under his thumb.

FINANCE

All governments need to have money before they can do much and this was Napoleon's first problem. When he took control he found the Treasury empty. With his Minister of Finance, Gaudin, he built up a more efficient system of taxation. The power to collect taxes was given to a general director of taxation who had under him deputy directors for each Department. As a result people could not so easily get out of paying taxes and the collectors had to be more honest. The Bank of France was founded in 1800 to loan money to the government, to look after the money from taxation and to pay out pensions. But in the end, in spite of his reforms, Napoleon was never completely out of debt, as he needed more and more money to pay for his wars.

THE LAW

Napoleon turned next to the laws. France desperately needed one set of laws to settle disputes about property. At the time there were some 366 different sets of laws in force. Moreover, the Revolution had made a lot of problems about property by sweeping away the special rights of the nobility and by taking over Church lands. In this work Napoleon continued what the various Revolutionary Governments had begun. The *Civil Code* which was issued in 1804 and renamed the Code Napoleon in 1807, was an example, therefore, of Napoleon completing the work of the Revolution. Lawyers did most of the work in making the Code, but Napoleon pushed it through. The lawyers who made the Code had a problem: how to keep people equal as the Revolution had tried to make them, and yet to give real power to the middle classes who would keep law and order.

So the Civil Code was a *compromise*. On the one hand, it had some of the ideas of the Revolution. There was to be liberty for each person, people of all classes were to be treated

25

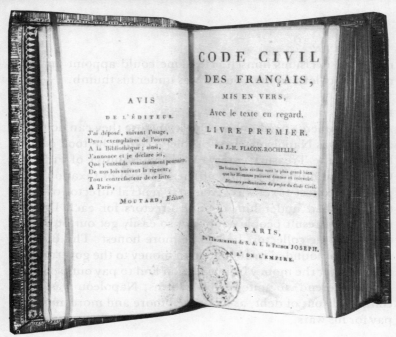

The Civil Code

in the same way in the law courts, and everyone was to have religious freedom. On the other hand, it favoured mainly the middle classes and men of property.

EDUCATION

Napoleon also made reforms in education, but again his main aim was to use education to keep the people in order and to help the State rather than the individual. For example, he did little to improve basic education for all children, since he had no desire to educate the poor in case it might encourage them to want to change their position in life.

However, because he knew that France would need well educated leaders in the future, Napoleon did much more for secondary education. Every district was to have a *lycée*, paid for by the government and there were to be 6,400 scholarships to help boys attend them. The subjects taught in these schools were chosen because they would be useful to the pupils. They were French, mathematics, history, geography, science and some Latin and Greek. However, Napoleon showed his views about the position of women in society, for he did nothing about the education of girls. As he said on 20 February 1806:

> I do not think we need trouble ourselves with any instruction for young females; they cannot be brought up better than by their Mothers. Public education is not suited for them, because they are never called upon to act in public. Manners are all in all to them, and marriage is all they look to.

Napoleon planned to crown his educational reforms with a great University of France. It was started in 1808 as the Imperial University, to be as he said, 'a nursery for professors, rectors (priests) and teachers generally, and they shall be stimulated by high motives'. In March 1806 when he was planning the University, he made his aim clear. He said: 'After all, my chief object in establishing a body of instructors is that I may possess the means of directing the political and moral opinions of the community.' Thus, for Napoleon, education was mainly a means of teaching people to obey the government.

RELIGION

He thought of religion in the same way. He does not seem to have held any firm religious beliefs, but he knew that religion had great importance for society. He thought of it as a kind of cement which bound the people together, saying:

> How can you have order in a State without religion? Society cannot exist without inequality of fortunes, which cannot endure apart from religion. When one man is dying of hunger near another who is ill because he has had too much, he cannot resign himself to this difference, unless there is an authority which declares 'God wills it thus': There must be poor and rich in the world, but hereafter and during all eternity the division of things will take place differently.

What he meant was that people would put up with being poor in this world if they believed God would give them a better deal in the next. If the people needed a religion, Napoleon was certain that this religion must be in the hands of the government. During the French Revolution the Church in France had been destroyed; now Napoleon wished to make peace with the *Pope* and bring the Church back.

In July 1801 the Pope and Napoleon came to an agreement called the 'Concordat', and it was proclaimed with great pomp at the Cathedral of Nôtre Dame in Paris on Easter Day, 18 April 1802. Napoleon made his generals and courtiers all attend and take part. The Concordat said that the French government recognised that the Roman Catholic religion was the 'religion of the majority of Frenchmen', though freedom to worship was also allowed to Protestants and Jews. Napoleon was to choose all bishops and the French government would pay the salaries of all the clergy. The Concordat also said that Church lands which had been sold during the revolution should not be given back.

Napoleon had difficulty in getting the French people to accept the Concordat. If you read the Then and There book on the French Revolution, you will see why many of them had hated the churchmen. On the whole, Napoleon's Council and his generals were against it but Napoleon carried it through. He knew that many were against it but as he said in 1807: 'People may call me a *Papist* if they like. I am nothing. I was a *Mohammedan* in Egypt: I shall be a Catholic in France, for the sake of the people.'

In fact he thought all the work which he had done in France was for the sake of the people. Though he had taken all the power for himself he had made the government work much better, he had made a firm set of laws and he had given back to France the religion which most Frenchmen wanted. In this way he had brought peace and order to France.

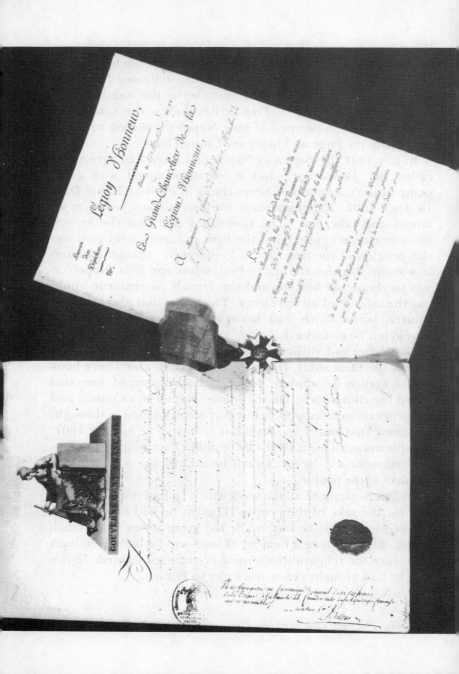

5   *Emperor of the French*

When Napoleon made peace with England (25 March 1802) it was hailed as a triumph in France and the Senate suggested that, to show how grateful the people were, they should offer him the Consulship for a further ten years. Napoleon replied by saying that he would accept if the people voted for it. So a *plebiscite* was arranged and about three and a half million people voted that he should be First Consul for life. Napoleon was home and dry. He had complete power. He gave the Senate great power and made sure the senators were his friends. Now Napoleon chose the men who were to govern; *democratic government* had gone. 'Liberty', one of the ideals of the Revolution, seemed to have disappeared from view in Napoleon's France.

The 'Legion of Honour' put the final touch to this. Napoleon wanted to bind people to himself by offering them high positions and honours, so in May 1802 he set up the Legion of Honour. Members were to be selected by a Grand Council, presided over by Napoleon himself. This Council granted different ranks to members, such as Grand Officer, Commander, and Chevalier, and gave a pension to each member according to his rank. Although many of his councillors opposed it, Napoleon had a ready answer for those who disapproved. When someone, for example, called the decorations 'toys', Napoleon replied: 'You are pleased to call them "toys". Well, it is with toys that mankind is governed.' In

Opposite: *The Cross of the Legion of Honour with the nominating letter on the right and the oath of loyalty on the left given to Francois Bécherel, Bishop of Valence on 6 July 1804*

some ways he was right. People will often obey a ruler who gives out honours and favours. Certainly the members of the Legion were likely to be his grateful supporters, but people who had been enthusiastic for the Revolution idea of equality felt that he was betraying this ideal.

Napoleon was now practically a king in all but name. However, there were still many royalists in France. In January 1804 it was discovered that a man called Georges Cadoudal had plotted with some of Napoleon's generals and some English ministers, to seize Napoleon and put a prince of the old royal

The execution of the Duke d'Enghien

family in his place. The culprits were imprisoned, but Napoleon became more and more worried by threats by royalists to kill him and so he decided to make an example.

When he heard that the Duke d'Enghien, one of the royal family, was in Alsace, plotting against him, Napoleon ordered that he should be seized in the territory of the Duke of Baden. On 21 March 1804, at three o'clock in the morning in the moat at Vincennes, the Duke d'Enghien was shot, on Napoleon's orders, as a spy in the pay of the English. His execution caused a great outcry, even in France. There was no evidence that he was in the Cadoudal plot or in the pay of the English, and in any case it was illegal to seize the Duke on neutral territory. For Napoleon, however, the execution was right for two reasons. First, it frightened royalists from plotting to kill him. Secondly, because Napoleon had now killed a royal prince, it was clear that there was no chance of the old royal family getting back again.

The way was now open for Napoleon to become a monarch himself and in May 1804 the Senate gave him the Imperial Crown. Shortly afterwards a plebiscite confirmed that this was the wish of the French people. Finally, on 2 December 1804, the Imperial Coronation took place, Pope Pius VII travelling from Italy to Paris for the occasion. Someone who was at the coronation left this account of it:

> The Pope preceded the Emperor by several hours, and showed himself wonderfully patient, sitting all this while on a throne that had been prepared for him in the church, without a murmur either at the cold or at the *tedium* of the hours that went by before the arrival of the procession. The church of Nôtre Dame was decorated with taste and magnificence. At the far end a stately throne had been raised for the Emperor, where he could appear in the midst of the whole court. Before leaving for Nôtre Dame we were ushered into the Empress's apartment. Our dress was very brilliant, but its *lustre* paled before that of the imperial family. The Empress especially, blazing with

diamonds, her hair in a thousand ringlets in the Louis XIV style, did not look more than twenty-five. Her sisters-in-law were also sparkling with an infinite number of precious stones, and Napoleon, inspecting us all one by one, smiled at this *opulence*, which was, like all the rest, the sudden creation of his will. He also was brilliantly attired. Since his imperial robes were only to be put on at the church, he wore a French coat of red velvet embroidered in gold, white sash, a short cloak spangled with bees, a hat turned up in front with a diamond clasp and surmounted with white feathers, and the collar of the Legion of Honour in diamonds. The entire costume suited him very well.

Napoleon took his place in a gilt coach with seven windows, along with his wife and his two brothers, Joseph and Louis. Then everyone *repaired* to the carriage *allotted* him, and the long *cortège* made its way at a walking pace to Nôtre Dame.

There were plenty of cheers as we went by. They were not the rapturous outbursts that might have been wished by a sovereign anxious for a *token* of his subjects' love, but they might content the vanity of a master with more pride than sensibility.

At Nôtre Dame, Napoleon remained some time in the archbishop's palace to don his ceremonial robes, by which he seemed rather crushed. His small figure melted away under the huge *ermine* mantle. A plain laurel crown encircled his head. He looked like an antique medal. But he was intensely pale, genuinely moved, and his eyes appeared to have a stern and rather troubled expression.

The whole ceremony was most impressive and beautiful. The crowning of the Empress excited a general stir of admiration, not because of the act itself, but she went through it so becomingly, she walked so gracefully to

Opposite: *Napoleon crowning the Empress Joséphine. This is a very famous painting by the French artist David (see page 54). It now hangs in the Louvre*

the altar, she knelt down with a motion so elegant, and yet simple, as to please every eye. The Pope, throughout this whole ceremony, had something like the air of a *resigned* victim, but resigned nobly of his own will, for a great and useful purpose.

We dined at the palace, with the grand marshal, and afterwards the Emperor wished to see those of his court who had not retired. He was gay, and delighted with the ceremony. He thought us all pretty, exclaimed on the way women are *embellished* by finery, and told us with a smile: 'You have me to thank, ladies, for being so charming.' He made the Empress keep her crown on, though she had dined alone with him, and he complimented her on her manner of wearing the *diadem*. At last he dismissed us.

With the Imperial Crown, Napoleon had added glitter to what was in fact a *dictatorship*. But France was happy. Frenchmen were glad that their hero-statesman should become Emperor. It seemed that Napoleon was right in thinking most of the French liked to be governed well more than they loved liberty.

6 Conquering Europe

Napoleon had been crowned Emperor of the French but he was not content with this. He wanted to make the French the lords of Europe. He planned to conquer England before turning to the rest of Europe because he thought England would be his toughest enemy. However, his invasion plans went wrong and so instead he ordered the Grand Army to march for Germany.

This was one of the most successful moves Napoleon ever made, for in the next two years the Grand Army brought him great success. Unfortunately, as he made this clever change of plan he also made a terrible mistake. Instead of leaving the French and Spanish fleets in Cadiz where they were under British *blockade*, but nevertheless safe, Napoleon ordered them to sail and attack Naples in Italy. Napoleon's admiral, Villeneuve, left Corunna on 21 October 1805 with thirty-three ships but on sighting Nelson's fleet of twenty-seven tried to about-turn to Cadiz. It was too late. Nelson caught them and wiped them out at the Battle of Trafalgar. (You can read about this battle in another Then and There book called 'Nelson's Navy'.) Only ten French and Spanish ships returned to port. No British ships were lost.

The Battle of Trafalgar ended Napoleon's hopes of invading England. He regretted this later but meanwhile he marched across Europe in a blaze of glory. He was crowned King of Italy in March 1805, he made Genoa part of France in June, and in Germany he made alliances against Austria. As a result Britain, Russia and Austria got together in a *coalition* against Napoleon.

37

The Grand Army marched from the Rhine to the Danube and then surrounded the Austrian army under General Mack from the rear. On 20 October 1805 Mack surrendered at Ulm. The rapid marching which had brought the French from Boulogne to the Danube in forty days, had brought hardship to the soldiers but also the reward of a crushing victory.

Napoleon was delighted. He was more than pleased with his soldiers and he issued a *proclamation* to them encouraging them to go on and conquer Europe:

> Soldiers! this success is due to your entire confidence in your emperor, to your patience in overcoming *fatigue* and discomforts of every kind and to your remarkable courage.
>
> But we will not stop here. You are impatient to commence a second campaign.
>
> The Russian army, which the gold of England has bought, we have to serve in the same manner. All I wish is to obtain the victory with the least possible bloodshed. My soldiers are my children.

This was fighting talk. It bound Napoleon's soldiers to him and spurred them on to greater efforts.

From Ulm Napoleon swept into Austria and entered Vienna on 14 November. He was anxious now for a knock-out victory to end the war; he was too far away from France for safety and the Russian and Austrian armies outnumbered him. So he pretended that his army was weak and hinted that he was about to ask for peace. He then trapped the Austro-Russian army into an attack at Austerlitz, on 2 December 1805.

On the day before the battle, Napoleon was full of ease and confidence. He seemed to know that if he won this battle he could turn the map of Europe whichever way he wanted. Someone who was there has left an account of how he spent the day:

> I have rarely seen Napoleon as cheerful, as contented as he was all that day. More than once I caught him rubbing his hands joyfully, as though saying to himself: 'I've got

them', or 'They shan't escape me'. This confidence was shared by the whole army.

Supper showed the influence of this happy frame of mind. The conversation was never brisker or more lively. As soon as the meal was over, Napoleon said:

'Let's go and see the Guards.'

Scarcely had we reached the line when Napoleon was recognised, and the men stood up at the sight of him.

We had hardly gone fifty paces when a bit of wood across our path made him stumble. But luckily we caught hold of him in time, and he did not lose his balance. Then the grenadiers, of their own accord, took the straw on which they were lying, twisted it up to provide something like torches, which they set alight, and then walked in front of us to light the general, making the air ring with their shouts. . . . All down the line torches were made, and each troop, as it were, took over escort duty from the one before. Then, as always happens at these moments of enthusiasm, what remained of the beds was soon ablaze. This demonstration was not without its risk, because of the cartridges. And so we kept on shouting to the men: 'Mind your pouches!' And luckily no mishap occurred.

The coalition army, now commanded by the Emperor Alexander of Russia himself, numbered about 90,000. Napoleon seemed to have only 53,000 but he brought up his generals Davout from Vienna and Bernadotte from the west and so had about 75,000 men without the enemy knowing. Napoleon also fooled the enemy by hiding his main strength in the centre in hollows in the ground. At the same time he kept his right wing weak so that the enemy would attack there and gradually weaken their own centre in doing so. When the enemy centre had been thinned in this way, Napoleon released his main attack from the centre under Soult, broke the enemy lines and turned to surround their left wing. It was Napoleon's greatest victory. The enemy lost some 27,000 men while the French losses were only about 7,000.

What was it like to be in the thick of the battle? One of Napoleon's generals gives us a good description:

> The Emperor ordered me to take two squadrons of cavalry and one of grenadiers. We dashed at full speed upon the artillery and took them. The enemy's horses were overthrown by the same charge, and fled in confusion, galloping, like us, over the wrecks of our own squares. In the meantime the Russians *rallied*, but with a squadron of horse grenadiers coming to our help I could then halt and wait for the Russian reserves. Again we charged and this charge was terrible. The brave Morland fell by my side. It was absolute butchery. We fought man to man, and so mingled together, that the infantry on neither side dared to fire, lest they should kill their own men. The bravery of our troops finally bore us triumph over all opposition. The enemy fled in disorder in sight of the two Emperors of Austria and Russia who had taken their station on a rising ground in order to be spectators of the contest. They ought to have been satisfied, for I can assure you they watched no child's play. For my own part I never passed so delightful a day. The emperor received me most graciously when I arrived to tell him that the victory was ours; I still grasped my broken sabre, and as this scratch upon my head bled a lot, I was all covered with blood. He named me general of division. The Russians returned not again to the charge — they had had enough. We captured everything — their cannon, their baggage, their all in short.

After the battle Napoleon toured the battlefield. General Savay left this account:

> The emperor came back in the evening, along the whole line where the different regiments of the army had fought. It was already dark: he had recommended silence to all who accompanied him, that he might hear the cries of the wounded; he immediately went to the spot where they

Opposite: *The Battle of Austerlitz, 1805*

were, alighted himself, and ordered a glass of brandy to be given them from the canteen which always followed him. He himself ordered a large fire to be lit near each of them, sent for a *muster-master* and did not leave till he had arrived; and having left him some of his own escort, ordered him not to quit these wounded till they were all in hospital. These brave men loaded him with blessings which found their way to his heart much better than all the *flatteries* of courtiers. It was thus that he won the affection of his soldiers, who knew that when they suffered it was not his fault; and therefore they never spared themselves in his service.

The next year Napoleon defeated Prussia at the battle of Jena and occupied that country as a base from which to advance against the Russians who were preparing to attack him. On 14 June 1807 he gained a decisive victory against the Russians at Friedland. Someone later recalled the enthusiasm with which the French troops entered the battle:

The march of the Emperor and his army was rapid, and the soldiers of the guard each felt personally engaged in the cause of the great captain!

All of them loved glory and went running to meet the dangers that *confer* it. And so this great and heroic army of 50,000 men, with Napoleon marching at its head, arrived before Friedland at 5 in the afternoon, all in one mass, without leaving behind a single straggler.

The battle however had its bloody as well as its glorious side, as the same person recalled:

Our infantry went in for a bayonet attack on the Russian Imperial Guard — every man a giant of the North — in the *ravine* encircling the town of Friedland. . . . It was the *pigmies* who beat the giants. Two hours later, as we passed through this ravine, where our horses had blood up to their *hocks*, we saw, before entering the town of Friedland, all the bodies of the grenadiers of the Russian Guard still almost in line where they had fallen, and almost all with their wounds in the chest; that was as high as our soldiers could reach with the bayonet. Each of those brave men had defended and kept his station. The battle had lasted 6 hours.

The Tsar of Russia, Alexander, immediately asked for peace and the two Emperors met on a raft in the River Niemen. Alexander seems to have been completely charmed by Napoleon. He not only made peace but changed his previous plans and joined the French. Napoleon even suggested to Alexander that France and Russia should divide Europe between them into east and west, Russia having the eastern part. Russia now promised Napoleon, in secret, to declare war on England and join the blockade of European ports to English ships which Napoleon had started.

Napoleon was at the height of his power. He had conquered western Europe and he now returned to his other aim — to conquer England. Now that he had conquered Prussia, Napoleon had control of the North Sea and Baltic coasts and this gave him the chance to beat Britain by blockade. In November 1806 he began the 'Continental System'. This put

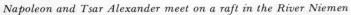

Napoleon and Tsar Alexander meet on a raft in the River Niemen

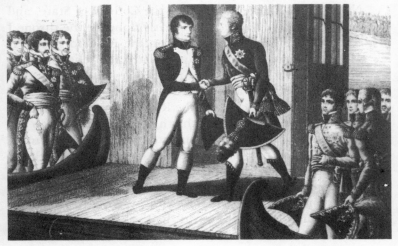

43

the British Isles in a state of blockade. All trade with Britain was forbidden and all goods coming from Britain or her colonies or being shipped to Britain were to be seized. Napoleon thought the British were a 'nation of shopkeepers', he saw that trade was Britain's life-blood, and meant to stop it and so slowly strangle her. At first it seemed that his plan would be successful. During 1808 British exports slowly went down. It seemed that nothing would stop Napoleon from becoming a world conqueror like those men of the past, such as Alexander the Great, Caesar, Augustus and Charlemagne, whom he so much admired.

This is a description of Napoleon as he was in 1807 at the height of his reign:

> With so many battles fought, so many victories won, so many obstacles overcome, and the triumphs of the *diplomat* added to those of the general, Napoleon left half Germany occupied by his troops. . . . He re-entered his capital on 27 July. His absence had lasted fully six months; he had never yet been away so long.
>
> This return was celebrated by public holidays, glittering with civil, military and religious display. Of these ceremonies, I particularly recall the *Te Deum* sung at Nôtre Dame. I attended it with the Council of State, and being placed in the *chancel*, nearly opposite the throne I could see the sensations shown on the Emperors face. It was obvious that he keenly appreciated the religious *sanction hallowing* in the eyes of the people, his glory and his *omnipotence*. He valued it all the more because, before then it had been lacking in the Revolution, and because it distinguished him from all that had gone before. I do not think there was any stage in his career when he *relished* more fully the favours of fortune. . . . A sword sparkling with gems hung at his side; the famous diamond known as the Regent formed the *pommel* of it. Its brilliance did not suffer one to forget that the sword was the heaviest and most triumphant the world had seen since those of Alexander and Caesar.

7 Life in France

Under Napoleon life in France returned to its old habits of the years before the Revolution. The revolutionary people, wanting all to be equal, had called each other 'citoyen' (citizen) and 'citoyenne' (for a woman), but now everyone went back to the old 'monsieur', 'madame' and 'mademoiselle'. Sunday came back and with it, officially on 1 January 1806, the old calendar which divided the year into twelve months. After the agreement with the Pope in 1801, church-going in the old way became popular again. It began on Easter Day 1802 when, to celebrate the alliance between France and the Pope, *mass* was said in Nôtre Dame Cathedral in Paris with grand ceremony. Napoleon and the other two consuls, Cambacérès and Lebrun, arrived in a procession of coaches which included *ambassadors*, ministers, and generals. The Cardinal-Legate said mass and at the most important moment in the service when the Cardinal *consecrated* the bread and wine the troops, lined up in the church, presented arms and the drums beat a general salute. Some of the generals openly laughed at the ceremony and afterwards in the evening when Napoleon asked General Delmas what he thought of it, he said: 'A fine piece of Church *flummery!* The only thing missing was the million men who gave their lives in order to destroy what you have just re-established.' Many felt like this, but gradually more and more people went to mass, not because there was a revival of religious belief but because it became the thing to do. If the Emperor went to mass, then all went as a sign of correct behaviour. He wanted religion to be a way of binding the people of France together.

Napoleon entering Nôtre Dame Cathedral, Easter Day 1802

Gradually high society also returned to its old ways. Once again people gave parties. In Paris, for example, the widow of a previous Duke of Orleans opened her household and men appeared there again in the shoes and silk stockings of a former time and footmen and servants put on the uniforms which the Revolution had forbidden. Here Napoleon and his wife Joséphine were to be seen at the regular Wednesday evening receptions.

An *aristocracy* also appeared in French society, though it was not quite the same as the old one. People did not get into this top rank because they were born noble but because Napoleon himself picked them out. He began with the Legion of Honour in 1802 and by 1808 it had 20,000 members. In

1808 a whole range of *hereditary titles* were given and the Empire had an aristocracy of 3 princes, 32 dukes, 400 counts, 1,000 barons and 48,000 knights. This new French aristocracy revolved round Napoleon just as the old French aristocracy had once revolved round Louis XIV. But these new nobles were different from the old in two ways. First, they had to pay taxes, from which the old aristocrats had been exempt. Secondly, a man had to have money to get or inherit a title under Napoleon's system: there was even a scale of payments so that each paid so much to become a count, so much to be a chevalier (knight) and so on.

Napoleon now began to hold a Court at the Tuileries Palace as magnificent as France had ever seen before. The Duchess d'Abrantes describes one of the many parties held there:

> On both sides of the room, three rows of women covered with flowers, diamonds and waving feathers. And behind them a line formed by the officers of the Emperor's household and those of the princesses; then the generals in uniforms glittering with gold, the senators, the councillors of state, the ministers all richly dressed, their breasts covered with stars and ribbons.

Napoleon's rule also brought a return to older fashions of men's dress. He disapproved of the wearing of uniforms at dances and gradually men began to wear the elegant, brightly coloured and embroidered coats of the eighteenth century, with white satin breeches and silk stockings. This was a change from the crumpled, badly fitting, heavy cloth coats which men had been wearing since the Revolution in 1789.

On the question of women's fashion Napoleon was even more dominating. He would not let his wife Joséphine wear the flimsy, almost transparent, Grecian tunics which had been fashionable under the old government. Instead, with the help of Joséphine's dressmaker, Leroy, a new Empire fashion developed and soon all the ladies at Court followed it. Waist lines were high and dresses hung straight with short, puffed sleeves. They were made of *tulle* or of velvet and silk, which

47

A high society ball

Napoleon particularly recommended to help the industry of Lyons. There were no high heeled shoes and ladies wore thin *buskins* on their feet. Hair styles were very neat and fairly simple, though you were allowed to decorate your hair with ribbons and jewels. All in all, it was a fashion which showed women as they were. As someone said: 'Dressed in this way, an ugly woman becomes more so, a pretty woman looks prettier; a really beautiful woman scores a triumph.' In only one way could women artificially improve their appearance. Make-up was used generously. Napoleon, in particular, liked his wife Joséphine to be well plastered with powder and grease paint, and almost every year she bought more than 3,000 francs worth of rouge.

Changes were happening in the furnishings of houses too. A new simple style, which copied *classical lines*, developed and

48

Empire style furniture

became known as the Empire style. Soon the large pieces of furniture in mahogany and ebony wood, with their carvings of crowns and lions' heads, and the tables supported on *griffins' talons* — all symbols of victory and triumph — appeared, not only in the houses of the rich but also in the homes of ordinary people.

Napoleon brought France other signs of riches and grandeur. The Louvre palace had been opened as a public museum in 1793 before Napoleon's rise to power, and various works of art had been stolen from Belgium and Holland before he took command of the army of Italy. However, after 1796 the flow of art treasures to France increased by leaps and bounds. On his campaigns in Italy, Germany, Austria and Spain, Napoleon took art experts who looked at the paintings, sculptures and rare books and manuscripts which they found

49

and sent the best of them back to the Louvre. As a result in 1803 the Louvre was renamed the Musée Napoléon and by 1814 had the most splendid collection of art that had ever been seen. Like one of the Roman Emperors of the past, Napoleon brought back to France these treasures from his conquests for the people of France to enjoy, and the French were delighted and proud to have them.

Living in Paris under Napoleon meant living with much dirt and poor services. Paris was a crowded city and Napoleon began to rebuild and replan in order to make more space in the capital city of France. However, his plans were so ambitious that they were not carried out for a long time and meanwhile Parisians lived in what must have seemed like a huge builders' yard. In time four new bridges were built across the River Seine and long stretches of new embankments made. Pavements were made for many streets and the area around Nôtre Dame was cleared of the buildings which hemmed it in.

But Paris remained a very dirty city. Unlike London it had few pavements and pedestrians had to walk as close to the walls of buildings as they could to avoid being run over. When it rained the flagstone streets, paved with uneven stones and with a central gutter, became swamps of mud and water. The main trouble with Paris was that it had no proper water supplies. A few houses had wells in their courtyards and there were about sixty public drinking fountains, but you had to pay to use these and they often ran dry. Parisians mainly relied on the 'Auvergnats' who pushed their carts with water barrels round the city. These were supposed to contain pure water but often they had been filled from the Seine and the river was the main dumping ground of Paris. Napoleon took steps to change this. He built reservoirs which in time gave a sufficient supply of drinking fountains for the city.

In one other way Napoleon followed the example of the Roman emperors whom he so much admired. Like them he saw that his Empire must be linked by a good road system and this he provided. For highly secret messages a *courier* service could get a message to Milan and an answer back in eight days and from Naples in fifteen days. For more ordinary business a series of signal stations, some eleven to twelve kilometres apart could send messages by semaphore, and this could be done even at night if the signallers attached lanterns to their arms.

Canals were another means by which Napoleon tried to unite the territories he ruled. In 1808 there were 800 kilometres of canals in France. Napoleon added almost 2,000 kilometres more and so joined all the main river systems of France. As a result coal and food could be brought to all the main cities of France. Napoleon knew full well that one way to keep people's minds off politics was to keep them well fed and prosperous. Better roads and canals were as much a part of his concern to keep people contented as were his plans for agriculture and industry. In 1803 he started local chambers of manufacturers to make people produce more goods. His wars also made it necessary to increase the manufacture of cloth and iron. For the trade war against British cloth imports encouraged the growth of French factories and by 1815 there were about 40,000 cotton workers in France and over 50,000 linen workers. More coal and iron was produced and workers were kept busy making arms for the army.

But French industry under Napoleon did not really grow very fast and trade was almost brought to a standstill by the blockade against Britain and her allies. Farmers were encouraged to grow more wheat, potatoes and beet by agricultural societies which gave prizes. Napoleon once said: 'I fear riots caused by a shortage of bread more than a battle against 200,000 men.' So he tried to make sure that there was always a reserve store of flour to be used in times of bad harvest. This succeeded fairly well until 1811-12 when things got bad. Some dealers began hoarding flour to put the price up. Napoleon tried to fix a maximum price for corn and also to force farmers to declare the amount they had produced, but his plans failed. He did not dare to try bread rationing for fear of setting people against him and it was only the better harvests of 1812 which saved the situation.

Though people were sometimes afraid of being hungry, they were often more afraid of police and prisons. As well as the glory and the improvements which Napoleon brought to France, he also brought a police state. The Ministry of Police had been abolished in 1802 but it was revived in 1804 and some people were imprisoned without trial or tried without a jury. Secret agents and spies were everywhere and men had to be careful that they did not talk loosely about Napoleon's way of ruling. The jails were full and the prison ships busy taking prisoners to the French penal colony of Guiana in South America. After 1807 many theatres were closed and those that remained open could only use plays approved of by government officials, and they were watched by the police. There was also a close *censorship* of the press. Local newspapers were all controlled by the government. In 1810 Napoleon tightened up his control over books when he set up a special office to watch over printing and bookselling. He gave money to artists and writers but they were not allowed to say or paint what they liked. For example, Jacques Louis David was named 'painter to the government' with authority over all paintings done in France. Many of his own paintings were magnificent but usually they were painted to glorify Napoleon and his rule. As for writers, the most creative, such as Chateaubriand and Madame de Staël, were both critics of the Empire. Napoleon ruled by fear and power. As one of his officials said: 'You are my friend. But if the Emperor ordered me to throw you into the river at noon, you would be there at a quarter to.' Napoleon knew that people would put up with their loss of freedom so long as they were rich and victorious. In 1807 there seemed no reason why he should not continue to give the French both victories and riches.

54 *Napoleon crossing the Alps, another painting by David*

8   Napoleon's Army

Napoleon's empire was won by his army and depended on it. Without his soldiers Napoleon would have been nothing. He well knew this and for this reason between 1801 and 1805 he thoroughly re-organised the French army.

All Frenchmen between the ages of twenty and twenty-five could be called to do military service, though to save the expense of providing relief for wives and children, married men with children could be let off. Naturally enough this led to many hasty marriages! After 1806 the prefects in the departments drew up a list of possible recruits and chose them by lot. However, it was possible for a recruit to get a volunteer or a paid substitute to go in his place. So the wealthier people could buy themselves out of the army and the main burden fell on the poor who could not afford substitutes. Not surprisingly, the poor came to hate military service, particularly after 1805 when France was almost continually at war. 'Conscripts need not spend more than eight days in training camps', wrote Napoleon. Raw recruits picked up some necessary information on the way to the battlefield and the rest they learned by mingling with the veterans in the regiments to which they were sent. They came back home only when they were too badly wounded to fight any more.

There was no drilling, and discipline was bad. Officers were drawn mainly from the ranks and in fact little notice was taken of rank, since an officer might well have been a comrade the day before. There were mutinies but on the whole Napoleon did not worry. He regarded his soldiers basically as fighting men and not as drill puppets. If they obeyed in battle and were eager to get at the enemy this was all he wanted.

There was also a feeling of freedom and independence among the men. Promotion depended on merit and success in battle rather than class or wealth. After a battle, the colonel of a regiment would fill the places of the dead officers by men who had fought the most bravely. Napoleon chose his generals in the same way and so the army offered a great chance to ambitious young men. As a result both officers and men showed in battle a daring of a kind which history had not often seen before.

Above all, Napoleon's armies showed a feeling of pride at belonging to 'La Grande Nation' and there was a common spirit — a *fraternity* — amongst officers and men which made them stand and fight together in an inspired way. Napoleon fed this spirit with his speeches to his soldiers, reminding them of the glory they were bringing to France. He also increased their personal desire for honour and glory by distributing ceremonial *muskets* and *sabres*. In 1800 a sergeant of grenadiers, named Leon Aune, received one of these sabres in the first distribution. He wrote to thank Napoleon, who used this very cleverly. He dictated the following letter to Aune:

> I have received your letter, my brave comrade, you had no occasion to remind me of your gallant behaviour; you are the bravest grenadier in the army, since the death of the brave Benezete. You have received one of the hundred sabres which I have distributed, and all agree that none deserves it better.
>
> I wish to see you again. The minister of war sends you an order to come to Paris.

As Napoleon had foreseen, the letter to Aune circulated through the whole army, and made the soldiers even more eager to win Napoleon's praise. Just think of it, the First Consul, as he then was, the greatest general of France calling a sergeant his brave comrade! This was true equality, and 56 nothing else was needed to rouse the enthusiasm of the army.

A grenadier
in the
Imperial Guard

A sapper
in Napoleon's
army

Napoleon followed this by distributing medals of the Legion of Honour and by granting distinctive uniforms to certain companies such as the Imperial Guard, which became personally attached to him and was the mainstay of his forces throughout his rule.

Napoleon also took pains to make his soldiers think that he knew them personally. When he was going to review troops he would ask one of his aides-de-camp to find out from the colonel of one of the regiments whether he had a man who had served in one of the campaigns in Italy, Egypt or Germany, what his name was, where he was born, the details of his family and what he had done. He would also find out which company he belonged to and his precise position in the ranks. Then Napoleon could at a single glance pick out the man who had been described to him. He would go up to him as if he recognised him, address him by his name and say 'Oh! So you 57 are here! You are a brave fellow — I saw you at Aboukir — how is your old father? What! have you not got the cross? Stay, I will give it to you.' Then as Napoleon's secretary, de Bourrienne, recalls:

> The delighted soldiers would say to each other 'you see the emperor knows us all; he knows our families, he knows where we have served'. What a stimulus was this to soldiers, whom he succeeded in persuading that they would all, some time or other, become marshals of the empire.

Napoleon's army was victorious because the soldiers would dare anything for such a leader.

There was little new in the way Napoleon arranged his army. The infantry remained divided into line and light infantry and no one invented new methods of fighting. The cavalry was better trained and was divided in 1803 into light cavalry (hussars), line cavalry (dragoons) and heavy cavalry (cuirassiers). In addition there were companies of horse and foot artillery. Napoleon's troops used a musket first made in 1777 which could fire four balls every three minutes and was accurate up to 180 metres. His cannon shot solid balls of 9, 18 or 27 kilograms at a rate of two a minute and their range was 550 metres. Napoleon regarded his artillery as very important but he never managed to get many cannon. Shortage of tools at home meant that the French never produced enough guns and even if they had, there was never enough transport to bring the guns and ammunition to the front. In 1808 there were only about two field guns for each thousand men and after this there were even fewer.

Bands played an important part in the army. They controlled its daily life; waking it up, announcing meal times and calling it together for orders. On the march, the drums kept it going. In battle, too, drum beats opened up the columns on the march, and drums and trumpets sounded its orders, such as the charge, the retreat and the rally, all when the noise of musket fire drowned the human voice.

A cavalry charge

In 1805, when Napoleon named his troops 'La Grande Armée' before the march on Germany, his army was the best in the world. Almost a quarter of the soldiers had been in previous campaigns and almost all of the officers had fought before.

However, weaknesses gradually appeared. First, as the war went on, the number of raw recruits increased. After 1809 some divisions were made up entirely of recruits. Secondly, the army changed from being all French and more and more foreigners were recruited. By 1812 there were fewer Frenchmen than foreigners in the Imperial Army which contained Italian, Dutch, south German, Swiss, Polish, Hanoverian and Irish regiments. Thirdly, when Napoleon began to fight in several places at once, he discovered that few of his lieutenants were able to take command in his absence. Fourthly, as conquests were made Napoleon moved too far away from France and this weakened his power greatly. There was too much to defend and his armies at the fronts were too far away from the centre and from each other to be strengthened.

Napoleon's soldiers received 5 *sous* per day and a bread and meat ration. However, this pay was not given regularly and it 59

Soldiers living off the land

was often overdue. When away on a campaign the soldiers lived off the land for their food, shoes and clothing; that is to say, they snatched what they could get. Napoleon relied on rapid forced marches and lightning attacks so much in his warfare that often his soldiers marched ill-prepared, with only one pair of shoes and what bread they could carry. As the wars dragged on, army supplies got worse. In 1814 Napoleon wrote to his Quartermaster, Daure:

> The army is dying of hunger: all your reports that it is being properly fed are pure moonshine. Twelve men have been starved to death, though every place on the road has been given over to fire and sword to extract food. And yet if I am to believe your reports the army is being properly fed. The cavalry of the Guard are dying of hunger. . . . Let me have returns of the amount of rice in the different army corps, but let it be an accurate report — don't double the figures of the stock in hand.

When supplies failed, the army suffered in three ways. First, it meant that the soldiers were badly fed, diseased and often exhausted. There were too few medical staff to deal with either the illnesses they got from living in filthy places or the wounds they got in battle. Between 1800 and 1815 about one million soldiers were lost, either dead or missing, about 40 per cent of the total. Of these only a small number died fighting. Most died from wounds and diseases and from exhaustion and exposure to the cold. Secondly, because the armies hadn't enough food, they were unpopular with the countries they occupied. Because they plundered and snatched whatever they could get, the people whose lands they crossed became their enemies. Thirdly, these armies could survive only so long as Napoleon waged war in fertile countries, as he had done in Italy. Once he invaded countries like north Germany, Spain and Russia where food was scarce his soldiers could not live off the land and his armies were in danger of being destroyed.

Napoleon could fight in many different ways, and on the whole his *tactics* were very successful. On the actual battlefield he tried to engage an enemy along an entire front so that he exhausted the enemy's reserves, while using as few troops as possible and keeping his own reserves fresh. Then he would try to break the enemy at certain points with continual infantry and artillery fire and by threats on their *flanks*. Finally, when he thought he had weakened the opposition, he would hurl in his fresh reserves and then pursue the beaten enemy without mercy.

This way of fighting battles worked in Italy and southern Germany, where the mountains and rivers hemmed in an enemy. But when Napoleon moved into Spain or on to the vast plains of north Germany, Poland or Russia this plan failed because he could not surround his enemy or even find them, and his armies had to make long forced marches. You will see how this happened in the next chapter, which tells about what happened to Napoleon in Spain.

9   The Spanish Affair

Napoleon was a man of simple tastes, normally content to wear a simple blue uniform. He ate and drank little and rarely spent more than a quarter of an hour over a meal. He seemed to live on work, 'Work is my element,' he was to say later, 'for which I was born and fitted. I have found the limits of power of my legs and eyes: I have never discovered those of my power to work.'

One secret of his success was his great energy and will-power. He wrote so many letters that they now fill thirty-two volumes! It has been worked out that he dictated about 80,000 letters and orders during his rule — an average of fifteen a day. The other secret of his success was his ability to inspire others. As we have seen, he talked with his soldiers and in battle his presence was always obvious. He had the knack of being friendly without making himself a fool. He had his reward, for his soldiers and his servants adored him.

Energy and ambition had brought Napoleon an Empire by 1807. Now they pushed him on to attempt more. He became determined to defeat Britain by his Continental blockade (known as the Continental System). The ports of Europe were closed to British goods and similarly it was forbidden to trade European goods to Britain. For about a year this plan seemed to work. Though there was a great deal of smuggling, the British were able to export much less to Europe. On the other hand, the Continental System hurt Europe as well as Britain. Trade and industry throughout Europe began to suffer. The Russians became angry that they could not sell their *timber* and *hemp* to Britain. Portugal was anxious to continue its wine trade with England. Sweden and Denmark sided with Britain, and Turkey signed an agreement with her. Napoleon's Empire began to crack like some huge building, and no sooner had he sealed up one crack than another appeared somewhere else.

The crumbling process began with the Pope in 1808. The Concordat had never been an easy alliance and when the Pope refused to join the blockade Napoleon occupied the Papal States and finally in 1809 annexed them. The Pope was arrested and imprisoned in Savona; not until 1814 did Napoleon allow him to return to the Vatican.

The next crack appeared in Portugal and in October 1807 Napoleon sent Junot with an army to conquer it. This brought French armies under Murat into Spain. Napoleon now had a vision of adding Spain to his Empire. He forced the Spanish royal family to give up their throne. On 7 July 1808 Napoleon's brother Joseph was crowned King of Spain.

The Spanish people were not prepared to take this lying down. *Rabble* armies were built up in many of the provinces

A British cartoon making fun of Napoleon's Continental blockade

and for a time they had unexpected successes against the French.

For example in June 1808 a French corps of 20,000 under General Dupont was attacked as it marched south into Andalusia and stragglers and small parties were captured by peasant bands and cruelly tortured and killed. General René who was captured as he tried to join Dupont's main army was, according to one account, lowered inch by inch, into boiling water. It took a whole afternoon before he died.

Napoleon decided to stop this Spanish war before it became too big and so he ordered his Grand Army to leave Germany and go to Spain and he himself took command. By the beginning of November 1808 he was at Vittoria and as he marshalled his troops for the march on Madrid he let the Spanish know his views. He warned some monks, many of whom had led rebel bands, that if they were determined to meddle in military affairs, he would 'cut off their ears'. To the rest he was just as insulting: 'I am here with the soldiers who conquered at Austerlitz, Jena and Eylau. Who can beat them? Certainly not your miserable Spanish troops who do not know how to fight.'

He was as good as his boast. Spanish opposition withered away and on 4 December 1808 Napoleon entered Madrid with a magnificent conquering parade. His brother Joseph, the official King of Spain was appalled by the pillage and plunder carried out by Napoleon's troops. In fact, he tried to *abdicate* but Napoleon would not hear of it. Various estates were taken over as Napoleon's property. Fortunately for Madrid, the plunder was stopped by news that a British army had appeared near Valladolid. Napoleon moved north to meet it and, though ice and snow delayed him, by early January his army was in a position to trap the British, as another French army came down from the north.

At this point Napoleon heard from Paris that Austria was preparing for war, so on 16 January 1809 he departed for

Opposite: *The execution of civilians by the French in Madrid, painted by the Spanish painter Goya*

France leaving Joseph in command of the army in Spain. On the same day the French fought the British at Corunna and most of the British army escaped by sea. Napoleon had hoped to return to Spain but in fact he never did. On the other hand the British did return and the speedy conquest of Spain he had hoped for was never completed. Instead Spain became a source of trouble for him which he could not cure. As he said afterwards, 'the Spanish *ulcer* destroyed me.'

Why were the Spanish so much against Napoleon? Under Joseph's rule they were given better laws in the Code Napoleon, such as trial by jury in open courts. The rights of lords and rich churchmen were taken away, so that the mass of the people were better off. Napoleon thought that this would keep them happy. In fact, however, Spain was still a country where the mass of the people were peasants who had been used for centuries to looking to their priests and nobles and kings for leadership, never questioning whether they were good leaders or not. Such people were not interested in having more say in their government. What did upset them was the taking away of their king. This hurt their pride and so they quickly responded to the local priests who organised the resistance to the French soldiers. So Napoleon found himself fighting a war in Spain where there was too much against him.

In 1809 the British General Arthur Wellesley drove Soult out of Portugal and won the Battle of Talavera. For this he was made Duke of Wellington, but he was unable to invade Spain until 1812 when he beat the French at Salamanca, where the French were weakened by Napoleon's withdrawal of troops for his Russian campaign. In May 1813 the British began a campaign which finally swept the French out of the peninsula.

Wellington now had a large army and in June 1813 he caught Joseph and defeated him at Vittoria. Wellington continued the attack and he was able to advance across the Pyrenees to Toulouse where he ended French resistance in April 1814. You can read more about Wellington in Spain in a Then and There book called 'Wellington's Army'.

10 The Grand Empire

Napoleon had left Spain in 1808 to meet a threat of war from Austria. He did this successfully and defeated the Austrians at Wagram on 6 July 1809. The next day he wrote to the Empress Joséphine that 'The enemy's army flies in disorder, and all goes according to my prayers. . . . My losses are full heavy, but the victory is decisive and complete.' Though he had won Napoleon realised that the Austrians were resisting him with a new determination. The case of the Austrian student, Staps, brought it home to him. For Staps, who was arrested as he tried to present a petition to Napoleon, confessed that he had intended to kill him — such was his loyalty to Austria and his hostility to Napoleon. One of the French generals left an account of what happened:

The peace was dragging out, the negotiations were making no headway, Germany was still suffering.

A young man, led astray by blind love for his country, formed the design of ridding it of the person he regarded as the cause of its ills.

He presented himself at Schonbrünn on the 13th of October, as the troops were marching past. I was on duty. Napoleon was between me and the Prince of Neuchatel. This young man, named Staps, approached the Emperor. Berthier, thinking he meant to offer a petition, stepped in front of him and told him to hand it to me. He replied that he wished to speak to Napoleon. He was told once more that if he had anything to communicate, he must apply to the aide-de-camp on duty. He fell back a few steps, repeating that he wished to speak to Napoleon himself. He advanced again, coming very close. I moved him back, and told him in German that he must withdraw. That if he had a request to make, it would be heard after the parade.

He kept his right hand thrust into a side pocket, under his great-coat. He was holding a paper, one end of which could be seen. He looked at me, and I was struck by his eyes. His determined air roused my suspicion. I called a gendarme officer who was present, and had him arrested and taken into the palace.

Everyone was intent on the parade. No one noticed.

Presently I was told that an enormous kitchen knife had been found on Staps. I informed Duroc. We both went to the place where he had been taken.

He was sitting on a bed on which he had laid out the portrait of a young woman, his pocket-book and a purse containing several old gold coins. I asked him his name.

'I can tell no one but Napoleon.'

'What did you mean to do with this knife?'

'I can tell no one but Napoleon.'

Were you going to attempt his life with it?'

'Yes, sir.'

'Why?'

'I can tell no one but him.'

I went to tell the Emperor of this strange event. He told me to have the young man brought to his closet. I transmitted his orders and went back. He was with Bernadotte, Berthier, Savary and Duroc. Two gendarmes came in with Staps, his hands tied behind his back. He was composed. Napoleon's presence had not the slightest effect on him. He bowed, however, in a respectful way. The Emperor asked him whether he could speak French. He replied confidently: 'Very little.' Napoleon instructed me to put the following questions in his name:

'Where do you come from?'

'Naumbourg'.

'What is your father?'

'A Protestant clergyman.'

'How old are you?'

'Eighteen.'

'What were you going to do with your knife?'

'Kill you.'

'You are mad, young man.'

'I am not mad.'

'Then you are sick?'

'I am not sick, I am in good health.'

'Why do you mean to kill me?'

'Because you are the *bane* of my country.'

'Have I done you any harm?'

'Me and all Germans.'

'Who sent you? Who is egging you to this crime?'

'No one. It was the deep-seated *conviction* that by killing you I should do the greatest service to my country and Europe which placed a weapon in my hand.'

'Is this the first time you have seen me?'

'I saw you at Erfurt, at the time of the interview.'

'Did you not mean to kill me at that time?'

'No, I thought you would not make war on Germany again. I was one of your greatest admirers.'

'How long have you been in Vienna?'

'Ten days.'

'Why have you waited so long to carry out your project?'

'I came to Schonbrunn a week ago, meaning to kill you, but the parade was just over. I *deferred* the execution of my plan till today.'

'You are mad, I tell you, or you are sick.'

'Neither.'

'Send for Corvisart.'

'What is Corvisart?'

'A doctor,' I answered.

'I don't need one.'

We awaited the doctor's coming in silence. Staps was *impassive*. Corvisart arrived. Napoleon told him to feel the young man's pulse. He did so.

'I am not sick, sir, am I?'

'The gentleman is in good health,' said the doctor, addressing the Emperor.

'I told you so,' put in Staps with a kind of satisfaction.

Napoleon, puzzled by so much confidence, began his questions again.

'You are an enthusiast, you will be the ruin of your family. I will spare your life, if you ask pardon for the crime you meant to commit, and for which you should be sorry.'

'I want no pardon. I am bitterly sorry to have failed.'

'The duce! it seems a crime is nothing to you.'

'Killing you is not a crime, it is a duty.'

'What is this portrait they found on you?'

'That of a young lady I love.'

'Your adventure will be a grief to her!'

'It will be a great grief to her that I failed. She *abhors* you as much as I do.'

'Well, but if I pardon you, will you be grateful?'

'I shall kill you just the same.'

Napoleon was *stupefied*. He ordered the prisoner to be taken away.

Staps was a nationalist, concerned to defend his country rather in the same way that the Spanish fought for their nation. One of Napoleon's mistakes was to forget the power which nationalism can give. Nationalism made both Austrians and Spanish stronger to resist the French, but elsewhere it caused him little trouble, partly because at first he seemed to be helping some nations against their foreign rulers. For example, in Italy he turned out the Austrians and made in 1802 the Italian Republic, and in 1805 a united Kingdom of Italy. Elsewhere it was a similar story. Holland was given to Napoleon's eldest brother Louis, though later it was joined to France.

Napoleon, then, was no friend to nationalism. He did not

Opposite: *Napoleon's Empire, 1810-1811, and the main battles 1807-1815*

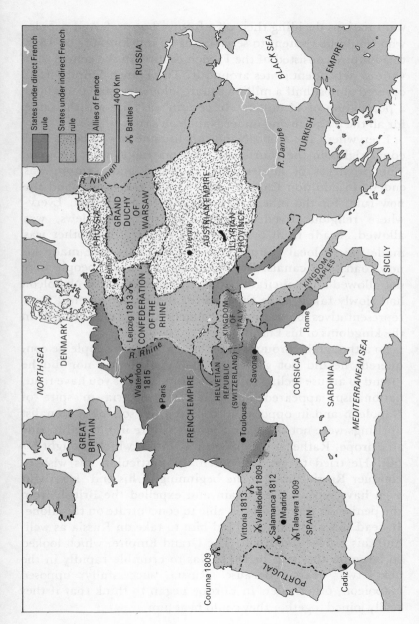

Legend:
- States under direct French rule
- States under indirect French rule
- Allies of France
- X Battles

400 Km

RUSSIA

BLACK SEA

TURKISH EMPIRE

R. Niemen

PRUSSIA

GRAND DUCHY OF WARSAW

AUSTRIAN EMPIRE

Vienna

ILLYRIAN PROVINCE

R. Danube

TURKISH

Berlin

Leipzig 1813 X

CONFEDERATION OF THE RHINE

SICILY

KINGDOM OF NAPLES

DENMARK

NORTH SEA

R. Rhine

Waterloo 1815 X

Paris

HELVETIAN REPUBLIC (SWITZERLAND)

KINGDOM OF ITALY

Savona

Rome

GREAT BRITAIN

FRENCH EMPIRE

Toulouse

CORSICA

SARDINIA

MEDITERRANEAN SEA

Vittoria 1813 X

Valladolid 1809 X

Salamanca 1812 X

Madrid

Talavera 1809 X

SPAIN

Corunna 1809 X

PORTUGAL

Cadiz

71

want nations deciding their own futures but preferred peoples who would be content to serve in his Grand Empire. By 1812 this Empire consisted of the French Empire in the centre with various dependent states around it. The French Empire itself covered almost half a million square kilometres and contained a population of 44 million. In certain ways life was the same for all the people living under Napoleon's rule.

Everywhere the Code Napoleon became law. People had equal rights in the courts and civil marriages were allowed. The privileges of nobles were abolished and *serfdom* was ended. In addition Church property was taken over and the new rules for the inheritance of property made law. Everywhere religious freedom, including rights for Jews, was allowed. Trade from one part of a country to another was made free of local customs duties, and plans were made for new roads and canals. But again, as in France, people were not allowed any policital liberty. We have seen how Napoleon had slowly taken away the right of the French to elect their representatives to government councils and he did the same in the kingdoms of his Empire.

So although he brought more equality to the people he conquered, he did not give them political liberty, nor did he intend to arouse feelings of nationalism. But, as you have read, nationalism appeared in Spain and Austria in spite of Napoleon and in opposition to him. Even so, the nationalist uprisings were not the reason for his failure in the end to rule all Europe. Rather it was his own ambition which brought his fall. He tried to get too much. In particular, his wish to conquer Russia brought the beginning of his end. He might even have reconquered Spain and expelled the British from the peninsula if he had been able to concentrate on this alone. Instead, his ambition tempted him to take on Russia as well, and this proved too much. The Grand Empire, which looked so large on the map in 1811, was to crumble rapidly in the next two years. Because Russia successfully opposed Napoleon, other rulers in Europe began to think that if they really joined together they could beat him.

11 To Russia and Back

The friendship between Napoleon and Tsar Alexander of Russia began to break down in 1808. One cause of trouble between them was Poland. Russia did not want a strong independent Poland again and it seemed to Alexander that Napoleon was rebuilding Poland in his Grand Duchy of Warsaw. More important was the fact that the Russians had never really accepted the Continental System. Many Russian nobles relied on selling timber to England for part of their wealth and this loss of trade annoyed them.

Finally in May 1810 Napoleon annoyed Alexander by taking over the Duchy of Oldenburg, when the heir to it was Alexander's brother-in-law. Alexander replied in December 1810 by putting high import duties on French goods and by opening Russian ports to neutral shipping. This was a direct break in the Continental System, which Napoleon felt he could not pass over.

General de Caulaincourt warned Napoleon not to move against Russia. He had been French ambassador in St Petersburg until February 1811. He recorded in his memoirs what Alexander said he would do if the French invaded Russia:

> If the Emperor Napoleon makes war on me, it is possible, even probable, that we shall be defeated, assuming that we fight. But that will not mean that he can dictate a peace. The Spaniards have often been defeated; and they are not beaten, nor have they submitted. But they are not so far away from Paris as we are, and have neither our

climate nor our resources to help them. We have plenty of room. . . . Your Frenchman is brave; but long *privations* and a bad climate wear him down and discourage him. Our climate, our winter will fight on our side.

Napoleon scoffed at this and said 'one good battle' would knock the bottom out of Alexander. But, in fact, it happened exactly as Tsar Alexander had said it would.

On 25 June 1812 Napoleon crossed the River Niemen with 450,000 men. (To follow his movements look at the map below.) At the start he had many more men than the Russians, whose two armies totalled in all about 160,000. The Russians could do nothing but retreat. Napoleon followed them, but his rapid advance stretched his resources. De Caulaincourt, Napoleon's aide throughout the Russian campaign, left this account of the situation:

This rapid movement without stores exhausted and destroyed all the resources and houses which lay on the way. The *vanguard* lived quite well, but the rest of the army was dying of hunger. Exhaustion, added to want and the piercing cold rains at night, killed off 10,000 horses. Many of the Young Guard died on the road of fatigue, cold and hunger.

Throughout July the Russians fought *rear-guard* actions which steadily cost Napoleon men. A Frenchman recorded

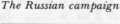

The Russian campaign

'that all the inhabitants had fled, leaving their houses absolutely deserted, and that everything went to prove that this *migration* was in accordance with a definite plan carried out under orders recently issued by the government'. At Vitebsk on 29 July Napoleon's generals urged him to halt the advance. The supply wagons and stores of all sorts which had been collected at such expense over the previous two years, had vanished. They were scattered along the roads, without horses to pull them or men to guard them. It seemed madness to go on.

But Napoleon pressed on. By 17 August he was at Smolensk. He battered the city with heavy artillery bombardment and forced the Russians to retreat but it was a hollow victory. All the Russians left him was an empty town on fire.

The Russians went on retreating and destroying by fire so that nothing was left behind them. Napoleon joked about this new method of warfare — 'a people who burn their houses to prevent our sleeping in them for a night'. It was no joke, however, for his soldiers, who found neither food nor shelter at the end of a day's march.

Eventually, the Russians did make a stand at Borodino. Napoleon still had more men than they had, 130,000 against the 120,000 under Kutusov, the Russian commander. But the Russians had heavier guns and a better defensive position. Nevertheless, Napoleon knew that it was a most important battle that he must win. On 7 September 1812 he issued the following order of the day to be read to the troops as daylight broke.

> Soldiers! This is the battle that you have longed for. Victory now depends on you: it must be ours. It will bring us abundance, good winter quarters and a quick return home. Do as you did at Austerlitz, at Friedland, at Vitebsk, at Smolensk; and may your conduct today be spoken of with pride by all generations to come. May it be said of you: he was at that great battle beneath the walls of Moscow!

Napoleon watches the burning of Moscow from the Palace of the Kremlin

It was a costly battle and the Russians were forced to retire. On 14 September Napoleon entered Moscow but it was empty. All had fled. Moscow was a deserted city except for a thousand or so poor people. The rich had left their great houses just as they were: 'Even the clocks were still going, as though the rightful owners were in occupation.'

That night some Russians who remained in Moscow set fire to it. The fire-fighting carts and pumps were found to be out of action. Eventually after five days the fire was controlled but not before the whole of the north west of the city had been destroyed, though the *Kremlin* itself had been saved. At first Napoleon thought he would spend the winter in Moscow but he found that there was just no food in the surrounding countryside. Meanwhile he sent letters and messengers to St Petersburg, hoping for peace talks with Alexander. However much Alexander might have wanted to make peace with

Napoleon he dare not. He knew that the French were bitterly hated after the miseries of the retreat which they had forced on the Russians. So no reply came back to Napoleon.

With no food, with no word from Alexander, on 19 October 1812 Napoleon decided to retreat to Smolensk, where he had left a garrison and supplies. The road was bad and sodden with rain and as he marched back snow began to fall on 3 November. Men silently dropped out of the marching lines to die of cold and hunger on their own.

We can get some idea of what it was like to be there on that terrible march back from Moscow from the memoirs of Sergeant Bourgogne. He began the march fairly happily, knowing that he had in his knapsack various costly presents which he had pillaged from the ruined city. He wrote:

> After getting past the rabble we were forced to wait for the rest of the column. I spent the time in making an examination of my knapsack, which seemed too heavy. I found several pounds of sugar, some rice, some biscuit, half a bottle of liqueur, a woman's Chinese silk dress, embroidered in gold and silver, several gold and silver ornaments, amongst them a little bit of the cross of Ivan the Great — at least, a piece of the outer covering of silver gilt, given me by a man in the company who had helped in taking it down. Besides these, I had my uniform, a woman's large riding cloak, then two silver pictures in relief, a foot long and eight inches high . . . all in the finest workmanship. I had, besides, several lockets and a Russian Prince's *spittoon* set with brilliants . . . also had a pouch full of various things, amongst them a *crucifix* in gold and silver and a little Chinese *porcelain* vase. These objects seemed to have escaped the general ruin by a sort of miracle, and I still keep them as relics. Then there were my *powder-flask*, my fire arms and sixteen cartridges in my cartridge case.

All this was some comfort to Sergeant Bourgogne as he trudged on in the snow but every day brought some new

tragedy to his notice. For example, on 5 November on the road between Dorogobousch and Smolensk, Madame Dubois, the regimental barber's wife, had a fine baby boy. There was 20 degrees of frost and to protect him they wrapped him in a sheepskin. Two days later, when she unwrapped him at his feed time, she found 'the infant was dead and as stiff as a board'.

The cold was so intense that men took extra clothes wherever they could. This story which Bourgogne tells, was probably a common happening:

> We suddenly came upon a gunner of the guard lying right across the path. By him was another gunner stripping his clothes from him. We could see that the man was not dead, as his legs moved and every now and then he struck the ground with his fists. Without saying a word, my companion gave the wretched thief a blow in the back with the butt of his musket. We immediately *abused* him [the thief] violently for his barbarous conduct. He answered that, although the other was not dead, he very soon would be, as he had been quite unconscious when placed there to be out of the way of the artillery, and besides, he was his messmate, and if anyone had the clothes he was the right man.

The retreating army looked forward to reaching Smolensk, where they expected to find the stores left previously on the way to Moscow. Imagine the disappointment when they marched into the town only to find that most of the stores had been used up by the soldiers left to keep open the lines of communication.

On 14 November Napoleon left Smolensk, and his army followed. Soon the road was a sheet of ice on which even men could not keep their feet. Horses and carts slid all over the place and blocked the way. All the while, too, the columns of men were attacked by raiding *Cossack* bands. Once

Opposite: *The horrors of the retreat from Moscow*

Bourgogne himself was nearly lost. He became separated from his comrades and found himself wandering until he came upon a blockage in the road of carts and bodies.

Close to me I found a small hatchet, such as every company carries in a campaign. I tried to cut off a piece from one of the horses, but the flesh was frozen so hard that this was impossible. I had spent the remainder of my strength, and I fell exhausted but the exertion had warmed me a little. I had picked up with the hatchet a few pieces of ice, which I now found to be blood from the horses. I ate a little of it and put the rest carefully in my knapsack; and feeling stronger, I set out again trusting to God's mercy. Taking care to avoid the dead bodies I went on, stopping and feeling my way whenever a cloud passed over the moon.

Sergeant Bourgogne eventually found the main columns and he survived the rest of the march with other adventures but without a major accident.

On 3 December Napoleon reached Molodetchna. Here he heard that back in France General Malet was trying to overthrow him by announcing his death. Napoleon decided to return to Paris. He reached Dresden on 14 December and four days later was in Paris. Behind him the remains of his army in Russia struggled to safety. He had gone to Russia with 600,000 men. Only 30,000 came back!

Despite this Napoleon still showed confidence. According to de Caulaincourt he admitted on his arrival in Paris that he had made a mistake but he did not consider that all was lost:

I have been to Moscow. I thought to sign peace there. I stayed there too long. I had thought to gain in a year what only two campaigns could achieve. I have made a great blunder; but I shall have the means to *retrieve* it.

Opposite: *The French cross the River Beresina on the retreat from Moscow*

12 Defeat and Exile

Napoleon's hopefulness was not foolish. There was no reason early in 1813 why he should not have made peace and kept his throne in France. The Russians were not anxious to follow up their advance and the Prussians were not keen to take on France again. Austria was certainly prepared to make peace and leave Napoleon and his Austrian wife, Marie Louise, on the French throne. (He had divorced Joséphine in 1809).

Napoleon, however, did not want peace, because he still wanted to keep his Grand Empire. He called up conscripts and by April 1813 he had 150,000 men for a campaign in Germany. Russia and Prussia had been allied against France since February and it was against their combined armies that Napoleon moved in April. At first he won some remarkable victories but then the tide began to turn. Austria joined the allies and the news of Wellington's success at Vittoria in Spain built up their confidence. Gradually they gathered larger armies and began to close in on Napoleon from all sides at Leipzig in October 1813, with more than 320,000 men to Napoleon's 160,000. He could not withstand this and was forced to retreat across the Rhine with only 60,000 men.

The defeat at Leipzig meant the end of the Grand Empire. The allies, now agreeing with England not to seek a separate peace with Napoleon, began the invasion of France. Napoleon fought battles against them and defeated two allied armies, but behind his back Paris gave in, allowing Alexander to enter it at the end of March 1814. The allies refused to make peace

Opposite: *The Empress Marie Louise and her son the 'King of Rome'*

84

with Napoleon and on 4 April his marshals forced him to give up the throne. He was given the Isle of Elba, an island between Corsica and the mainland of Italy, with an income from the state for himself and his family.

On 20 April Napoleon said goodbye to his wife and child and also to his Old Guard. It was a moving separation which brought tears to many eyes. Napoleon, having explained the reasons for his abdication, ended with these words: 'Do not mourn over my fate: if I have determined to survive, it is to serve your glory; I wish to write about the great things we have done together.'

At Elba he began to keep a court in the old imperial style. It was not easy for him to admit that his career as a ruler was at an end. He watched carefully what was happening in France and Europe. The allies were quarrelling at Vienna, as they tried to resettle Europe after the changes he had made in boundaries and kingdoms. France was not taking kindly to the restored Bourbon King Louis XVIII. News of what was happening finally proved too much of a temptation for him. He decided to bid once again for power.

On 16 February 1815 he left Elba and landed at Antibes on the south coast of France. He progressed northwards to Paris, being welcomed on the way, particularly by the peasants and by the army, who deserted the Bourbon king and joined their old leader. On 20 March he was received in Paris by a madly cheering crowd.

At first he tried to make peace with the allies but they would not hear of it. An allied army gathered in Belgium and Napoleon hastily raised conscripts to meet them. On 15 June French troops marched across the frontier into Belgium. On 16 June he met the Prussians and forced them to retreat. But he did not destroy them and that was to prove a fatal mistake. He now turned to deal with Wellington and the British, who fell back to Waterloo. Here Wellington gathered his forces.

Opposite above: *Napoleon leaves his Old Guard*

Opposite below: *Napoleon escapes from Elba*

Wellington had 67,000 men and Napoleon 74,000 when the battle began on 18 June.

Wellington had massed his troops on the crest of a hill and prepared to defend rather than attack. He managed to repel repeated French attacks. Both sides made magnificent but mistaken cavalry charges which left the cavalry in the middle of the enemy, so that they were cut to pieces before they could get back to their own lines. Moreover, Napoleon himself was ill on the day of the battle and this seems to have affected his generalship. Certainly towards the end of the day he delayed too much in sending in his reserves against the British and this allowed Wellington time to repair the gaps in his lines. However, at this stage in the battle Napoleon was still hopeful of victory, particularly if Grouchy, who had been sent after the Prussians with 30,000 men could return to reinforce his guard. So at 7 o'clock in the evening Napoleon sent in his last attack. It was beaten off and the arrival in the field at about the same time of Blücher and the Prussian army — which Napoleon two days before had foolishly allowed to live to fight another day — finally sent the French army into retreat. Fleury de Chaboulon who was with Napoleon as a secretary has left a description of what happened:

The Emperor, satisfied, was repeating joyfully: 'They're ours! I've got them!' And Marshal Soult and all the generals likewise regarded victory as assured. Meanwhile our cavalry, worn out by considerable losses and unequal fights endlessly renewed, was beginning to lose heart and give way. The issue of the battle seemed to be growing doubtful. It was time to strike a great blow by a desperate attack.

The Emperor did not waver. Orders were immediately given to Count Reille to gather all his forces and hurl himself on the enemy's right, while Napoleon in person would make a frontal attack with his reserves. The Emperor was already marshalling his Guard in column of attack when he heard that our cavalry had just been forced to abandon part of the heights of Mont-Saint-Jean. He at once ordered Marshal Ney to take four battalions of the Middle Guard and make all speed to the fatal plateau, to support the cuirassiers who still occupied it. The harangues [speeches] of Napoleon fired every mind; the cavalry and some battalions which had been drawn into its retreat faced the enemy with shouts of 'Long live the Emperor!' At that moment a burst of rifle-fire was heard. 'There's Grouchy!' cried the Emperor. 'Victory is ours.' Labedoyere flew to tell the army this joyful news. He broke through the enemy to the head of our columns: 'Marshal Grouchy is here, the Guards are being thrown in! Courage! Courage! The English are lost.' Just then Ziethen's thirty thousand Prussians, who had been mistaken for Grouchy's army, carried the village of La Haie by main force, driving us before them. Our cavalry, our infantry, already shaken by the defeat of the Middle Guard, were afraid of being cut off and retired headlong. The English cavalry, taking advantage of the confusion caused by this sudden retreat, made a way through our ranks and brought their disorder and discouragement to a climax. The other troops on the right, who had already done all they could do to withstand the Prussian attacks, and had been short of ammunition for more than an hour, on seeing some squadrons in chaos and men of the Guard stampeding, thought all was lost and abandoned their position. This *contagious* impulse spread to the left in a flash, and the whole army, which had so gallantly carried the best positions of the enemy, became as eager to give them up as it had been zealous in seizing them.

The English army, which had been advancing as we fell back, and the Prussians who had not ceased to pursue us, swooped with one accord on our scattered battalions; darkness increased the turmoil and panic; and soon the whole army was only a chaotic mass, which the English and the Prussians overcame without effort and slaughtered without pity.

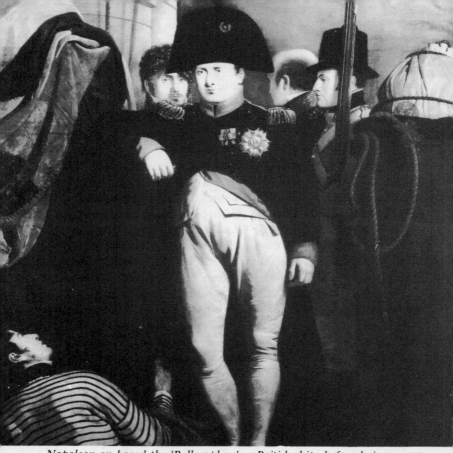

Napoleon on board the 'Bellerophon', a British ship, before being sent to St Helena

The Emperor, witness to this appalling *defection*, could scarcely believe his eyes.

Two or three hundred fugitives of all arms were rounded up to escort the Emperor. Along with General Bertrand, he got into a *barouche* and drove off.

You can read more about the battle of Waterloo in another Then and There book, 'Wellington's Army'.

This was the end for Napoleon. He returned to Paris but the French would not take him back as ruler. Eventually he gave himself up.

This time he was sent to St Helena in the South Atlantic and there he was kept as a prisoner until he died in 1821. He was not a silent prisoner. On St Helena he wrote his 'Memoirs' and also encouraged his companions to write down and publish what he said. Here he created what has been called the 'Napoleonic legend' — his story of his career. In it he said that he had always wanted peace and that the other rulers of Europe had forced him into war. He also claimed that in time he would have allowed nations to have their independence, and given people their liberty.

It is impossible to say what Napoleon might have done. People even have different opinions about what he actually did do. He can be praised for the good things he introduced in France: better roads, canals, new schools, equality in the law courts and tremendous glory for the nation. On the other hand, by the end France had her frontiers reduced to those of 1792, her colonies taken away, her finances weakened and her young men killed in the wars. Similarly it can be argued that he brought benefits to Europe: the Code Napoleon, equality in the law courts, the end of nobles' privileges and a beginning of national feeling in Italy, Poland and Spain, and particularly the German Empire where the number of separate states was reduced from 396 to 40. On the other hand, much of Europe had been pillaged, millions paid in taxes to France, European trade strangled for a while and over three million allied soldiers were lost in war and over one million French.

What can be said with certainty is that Napoleon was one of the most powerful men of action that the world has ever seen. A great soldier and a creative ruler, his restless ambition took him from the position of a French lieutenant to that of an Emperor of Europe. Many men dream of power. Napoleon had the energy and the luck to make his dream come true. Unfortunately for him, in the end he was too much of a dreamer and did not have enough common sense to know when to stop. He should have realised that the rulers of Europe, though they might allow him to rule a large French Empire, would never let him take over all Europe. But

A cartoon from Germany showing the rise and fall of Napoleon

Napoleon could not see this. For even if they had let him have Europe, he would have then gone on to want to rule more. Nothing would have satisfied him, for he had no final goal. He was like a hunter who would never stop, no matter how many animals he caught. For what he enjoyed was the chase, and the excitement of living dangerously.

There is one story about Napoleon which makes it clear that it was restless activity which he wanted, rather than any particular achievement. Some of his followers asked him what would satisfy him: 'Was it to be in God's place?' 'Ah!' replied Napoleon, 'I would not want it: even that would be a *cul-de-sac.*'

How Do We Know?

We know much about Napoleon from his own letters and writings. These were published by order of Napoleon III between 1858 and 1870 and they fill thirty-two large volumes. We also have the memoirs of many people who lived and marched with Napoleon: memoirs of important men such as Caulaincourt, Marmont, Pasquier and Rapp, and of ordinary soldiers such as Sergeant Bourgogne.

In addition, there are records about what Napoleon did, written in the languages of the various countries which his conquests affected — in German, Italian, Spanish and English. There are also paintings and cartoons by French, British and other European artists which help us to see how people thought about Napoleon.

All these writings and pictures come from Napoleon's own times. They are *contemporary* sources and are the best evidence for historians. There are also thousands of books which have been written about Napoleon since he died. Historians call these 'secondary' sources and these, too, help us to know about him.

Each book gives its own particular view of Napoleon and this book is no exception. It tries to give a balanced picture but, in the end, you will have to look at other books and make up your own mind about him. For as J. M. Thompson, one of the great English writers about Napoleon, wrote, 'there cannot be too many likenesses of a great man in the picture gallery of history'.

OTHER RELATED THEN AND THERE BOOKS
The France of Louis XIV
The Eighteenth Century Grand Tour
The French Revolution
Wellington's Army
Nelson's Navy

FILMSTRIP
Napoleon (Lives of Famous Men and Women: Common Ground)

Things To Do

1. Imagine that you are one of Napoleon's Imperial Guards and write, or tape record, an account of why you felt so much loyalty to him.
2. Imagine you are a young man who does not want to be recruited into Napoleon's army. Write an account, giving your reasons why and describing your adventures in avoiding recruitment.
3. Imagine you are a veteran who survives all Napoleon's campaigns. Produce a map showing your travels since you joined the army.
4. Listen to Tchaikovsky's '1812 Overture' with its imaginative description in sound of the Russian Campaign.
5. Find out more about some of Napoleon's battles and produce plans or models of them. (Airfix produce model soldiers of this period.)
6. If you have the opportunity, go and see the film 'Waterloo' — the exciting story of Napoleon's last campaign.
7. Debate the motion 'that Napoleon did more harm than good to France'.
8. Write or record an account of an interview asking Napoleon about his Spanish campaign and why it failed.
9. Write a newspaper article on the Battle of Waterloo as it might have been written by (a) a Frenchman; (b) an Englishman; (c) a Prussian.
10. Write or record an imaginary discussion between Napoleon and Alexander I of Russia discussing why their friendship broke down.

Glossary

to abdicate, to give up the throne

to abhor, to hate, dislike

to abuse, to speak insults

administrator, manager, director of an office

administrative districts, local government divisions

aides-de-camp, officers who wait on a general to carry out his orders or messages

allotted to: reserved for

ambassador, top diplomat representing his country in another

annals, historical records

archaeologists, people who study remains from ancient times

aristocracy, people with titles

Army of the Interior, the army based in France itself

artillery, part of the army which handles large cannon and guns

bane, cause of evil

barbarous, rough, uncivilised

barouche, coach

blockade, ships or soldiers preventing goods from reaching a place

buskins, small boots of soft leather

cavalry, soldiers on horseback

censorship, official watch kept in order to suppress any reports not approved by government

chancel, part of church near the altar

Civil Code, system of laws introduced by Napoleon, known as the Code Napoleon from 1814 on

classical lines, style of ancient Greece and Rome

coalition, two or more groups joining to work together

Code Napoleon, see *Civil Code*

compromise, agreement reached by each side giving way a little

to confer, to grant, give a favour

conscript, man doing compulsory service

93

to consecrate, to make holy, sacred

constitution, group of rules by which a country is governed

contagious, spreading of disease by touching

contemporary, coming from the same time

conviction, certainty

cortège, procession

courier, messenger

Cossack, skilled Russian horseman

coup d'état, sudden overthrow of government by force

crucifix, image of Jesus Christ on the cross

cul-de-sac, a road that leads nowhere and is blocked off

defection, desertion

to defer, to put off in time

democratic government, government according to the will of the people

Department, see *administrative district*

diadem, crown

dictatorship, government by one person with complete power

diplomat, person representing his country abroad

embellished, made beautiful

ermine, valuable white fur from an animal of the weasel family

etiquette, manners or rules of behaviour

fantastic, fanciful, improbable

fastidious, hard to please

fatigue, tiredness

fertile, fruitful, good for farming

flanks, two side camps of an army, left and right of the main camp

flatteries, excessive compliments

flummery, nonsense

fraternity, brotherhood

griffins' talons, the griffin was a fabulous animal with an eagle's head and talons (claws) and a lion's body

guillotined, beheaded by a machine known as a guillotine, named after its inventor

hallowing, making holy

hereditary titles, titles and offices which can be passed from father to son

hemp, raw material for making ropes which were needed for the sailing ships of that time

hock, joint of the hind leg, where it points backwards

impassive, unmoved, unresponsive

infantry, foot soldiers; divided into line units who kept together and light infantry who followed up with a quick charge

Islam, religion of Muslims, followers of the prophet Mohammed

Kremlin, citadel within the city of Moscow, containing the Imperial Palace

Legislative, part of the French government responsible for passing or rejecting laws proposed by the *Tribunal*

lustre, brilliance, shining splendour

lycée, secondary school

Mass, religious service

to massacre, to murder cruelly, kill without trial

migration, movement from one place to another

Mohammedan, follower of the prophet Mohammed, worshipping god as Allah

musket, light gun used by infantry soldiers

muster-master, officer responsible for checking numbers of soldiers

omnipotence, all powerfulness

opulence, richness

Papist, Roman Catholic, obedient to the Pope

pigmies, tiny people

plebiscite, the vote of a whole people on one particular issue

plundering, thieving

pommel, knob at the hilt (handle)

Pope, head of the Roman Catholic Church

porcelain, very delicate pottery

powder-flask, container for gunpowder

privation, hardship

proclamation, announcement

rabble, inferior or disorderly people

rallied, got together to resist again

ravine, narrow valley

rear-guard, troops at the back of an army

to relish, to enjoy

repaired, went (an old-fashioned word)

resigned, obliged but reluctant to give way

to retrieve, to win back

roubles, Russian coin

sabre, curved sword carried by cavalry soldier

sanction, authority

Senate, the smallest and most important group of people responsible for governing France *serfdom*, class of society where peasants worked for landlords

siege, operation of encamped attacking force to capture a fortified place

sou, least valuable French coin, worth about 2p in today's money

spittoon, bowl or jar to spit into

stupefied, amazed

tactics, ways of using troops in battle

'Te Deum', a hymn praising God

tedium, tiresomely long and boring

teeming, fully stocked

timber, wood

token, evidence, sign

Tribunal, committee of 100 members who discussed existing laws in France, but could not change them

tulle, fine silk net

ulcer, sore place

vanguard, the front or advance guard of an army

veteran, person who has served a long time in the army